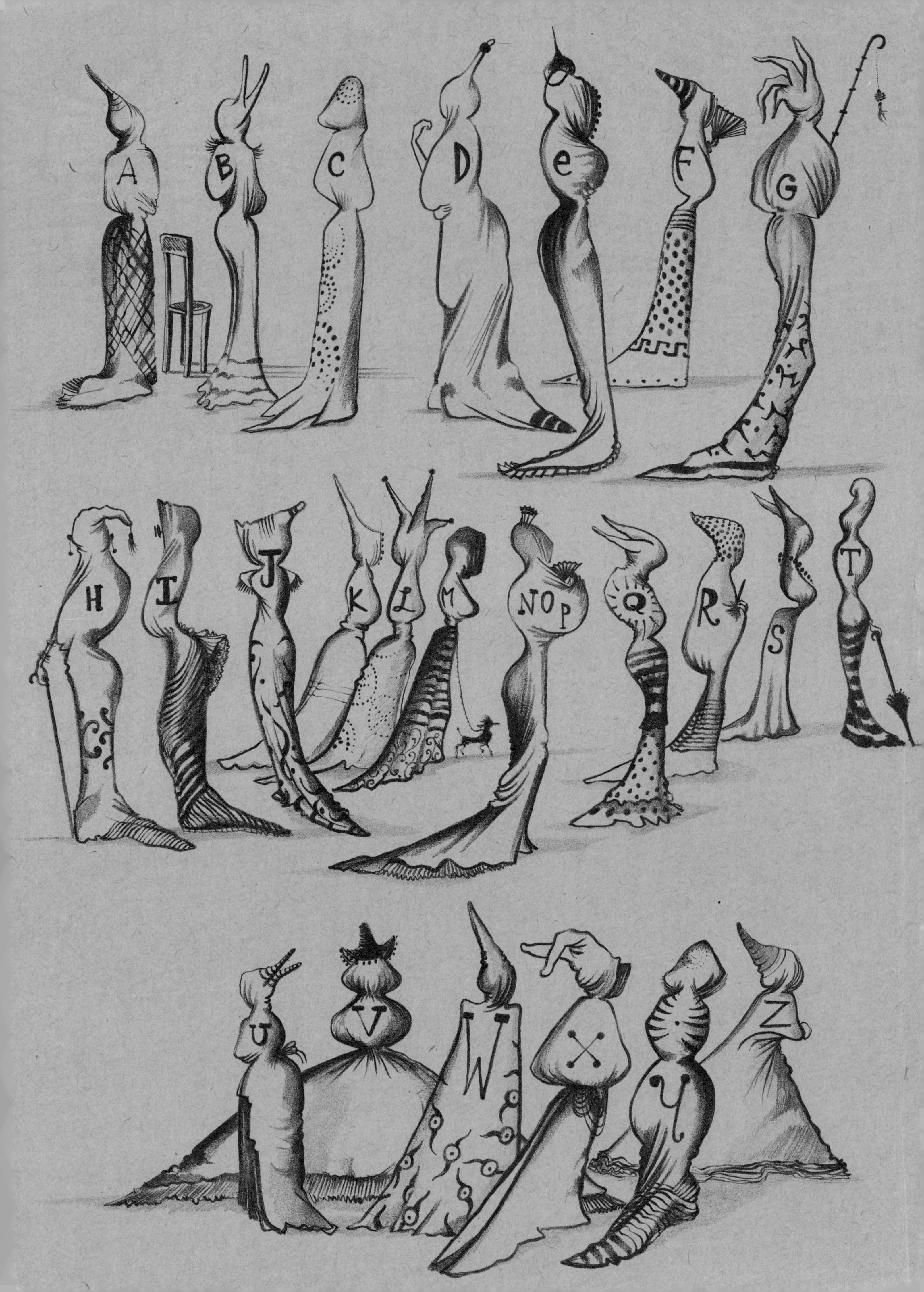
A
B
C
D
e
F
G
H
I
J
K
L
M
NOP
Q
R
S
T
U
V
W
X
Y
Z

STYLE
Dictionary
BY
Ruben Toledo

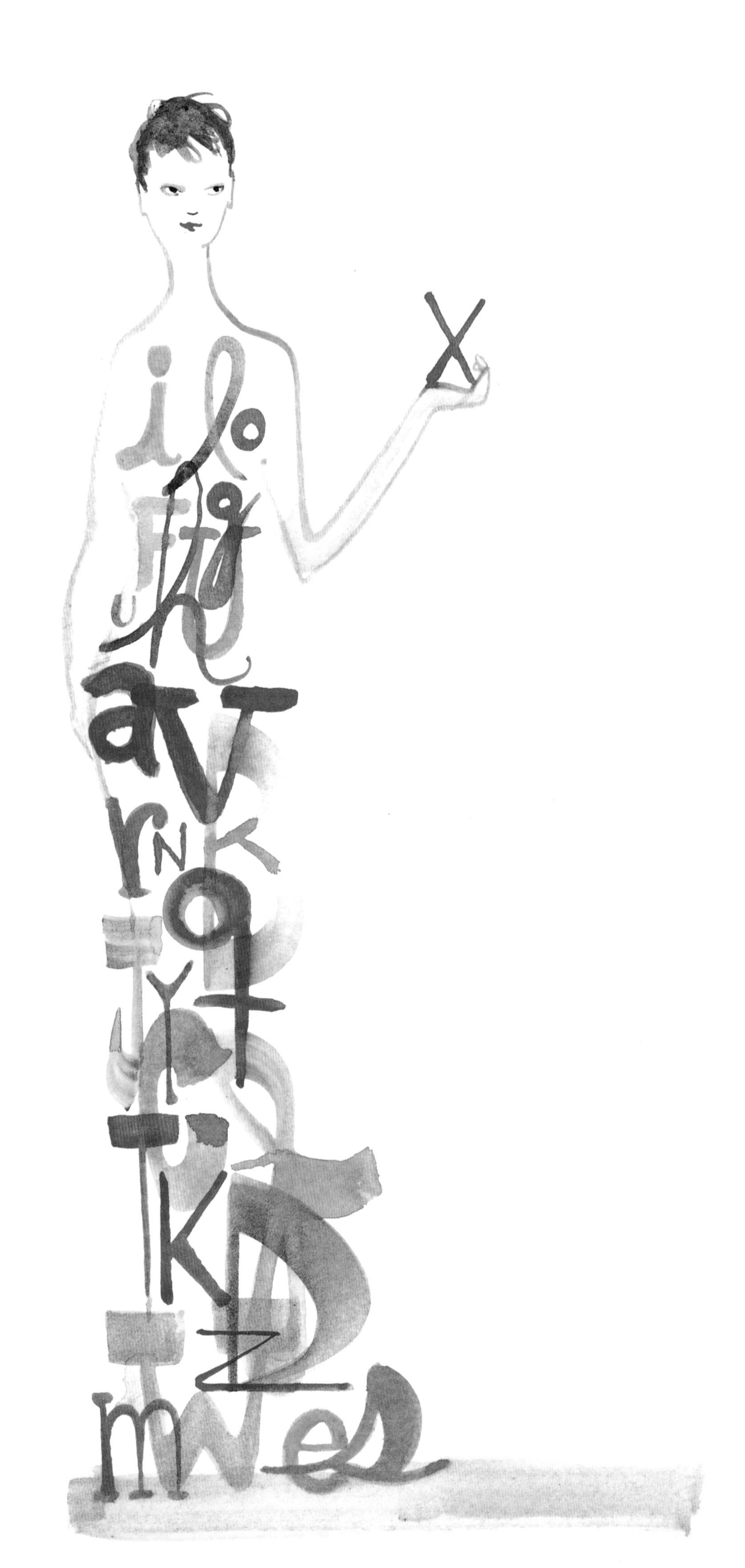

STYLE "DI,C-T;ioN(a)ry....?

; a VISUALIZATION — EXPLORATion — Transformation — MUTATION — DOCUMENTaTION — investIGATION — CLASSIFICATION — free-association — INTerpretation And exact QUOTations Of fashion TERMS and a collection of PAST WORKS by

Ruben Toledo

WITH AN INTRODUCTION BY Mr. RICHARD MARTIN

Concept Design by Mr. Juan E. Ramos

Of the 130 drawings in this book, 24 originally appeared in Details magazine; 4 in Visionaire; 10 in NEW YORK MAGAZINE; 2 in L'UOMO VOGUE; 2 in Elle magazine; 1 in Harper's BAZAAR; 2 in Vogue; 2 in Madame Figaro and 1 in Esquire Gentleman

acKNOWLEDGMENT AND THANKS ARE ALSO MADE TO THE METROPOLITAN MUSEUM OF ART COSTUME INSTITUTE, NEW YORK AND MUSEE DES ARTS DECORATIVES, PARIS

ABBEVILLE PRESS Publishers

New York London Paris

this **BOOK** is Dedicated to the MEMORY OF Juan Eugene Ramos and to my WIFE Isabel

INTRODUCTION

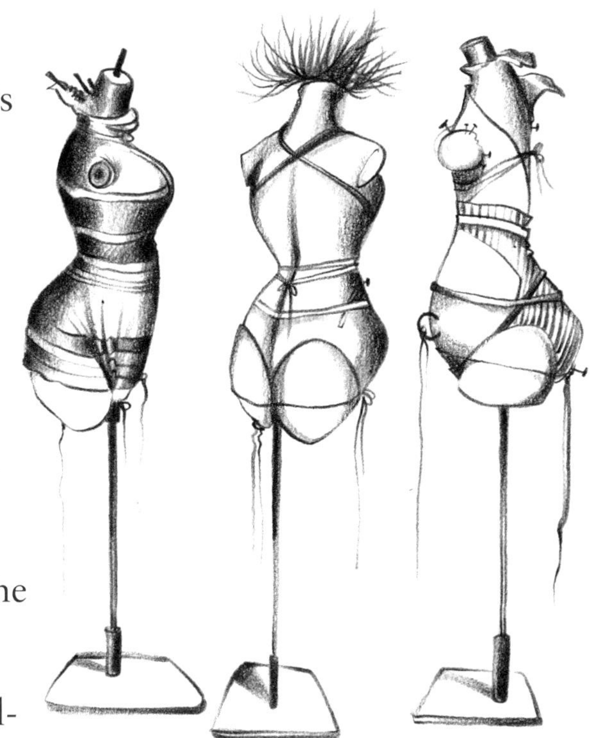

Style is elusive. One would welcome any glossary or manual to understand style. But Ruben Toledo's *Style Dictionary* is more than taxonomy or rudiments. Toledo shows us exactly what style is and has been with the most charming literacy of illustration and the most cogent observations on the world of fashion.

Toledo loves fashion, but he is also wonderfully cynical in the best sense of the *boulevardier,* the same role he assumes in life, walking amidst the fashion world with a dandy's fascination and poise. This Baudelairean hero imagines cities of silhouettes, veggy ladies in the tradition of Grandville, and wondrous wardrobes of sea, shell, idea, and armory. Toledo fulfills Baudelaire's critical concept of the possibility of reconciling the fugitive and the infinite. Toledo reports on a current style, on a magazine's re-direction, on images that we can identify to specific time and season, but each becomes an image and a perception more consequential than ephemeral. Toledo's compelling art is no mere document, though definitive—even in his whimsy of exaggeration and articulation—of fashion as we know it in the 1980s and 1990s. Toledo extrapolates from our time to style at its essence and style as eternal principles, rendering beauty, indulging excess, and bringing bodies into social and cultural metaphor.

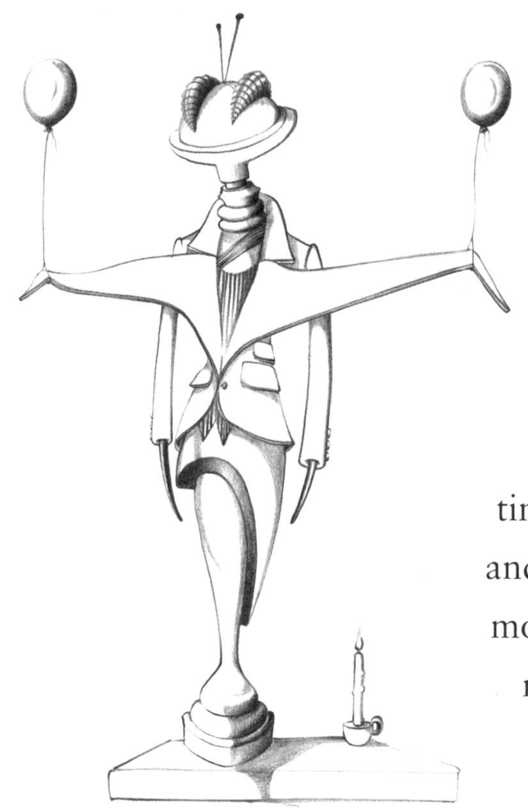

We are more accustomed in our time to making computer programs than dictionaries. The Diderots, Rogets, and Websters who made magnificent rosters of human behavior, objects, and words are of epochs long ago. Toledo's dictionary joins that wondrous series in which we are ever enlightened. The greatest fashion illustrator chronicling our time, Toledo is the artist who gives us the vocabulary and the unforgettable images that meld fashion at its most ephemeral and impressionable with style at its most abiding. The late twentieth century can be as proud of this book as the eighteenth century was of Diderot and the nineteenth century might have been of Daumier and dictionaries. Toledo's brilliant album portrays style in our time, but more importantly sustains style for all time.

RICHARD MARTIN
Curator of The Costume Institute
The Metropolitan Museum of Art

A
is for Afro-

Bb
is for
Bus·tle
dressmakers
homage
to
African
beauty

Bonnet
BeLT
Brassiere
Beard
Babushka
Bunny
Bikini

is for cor·set

Meet your new Consumer! — and How to spot her:

Neo-Joan of Arc

Neo-Globe-trotter/vamp

Neo-Revolutionary

C is for consumer

Neo-Bohémien

Neo-Conservetive

Neo-HouseWife

D is for Dress

E
eyeglass
earmuff
earings

conffessionals

HEAVY METAL

Pair of Screens

Rings of Saturn

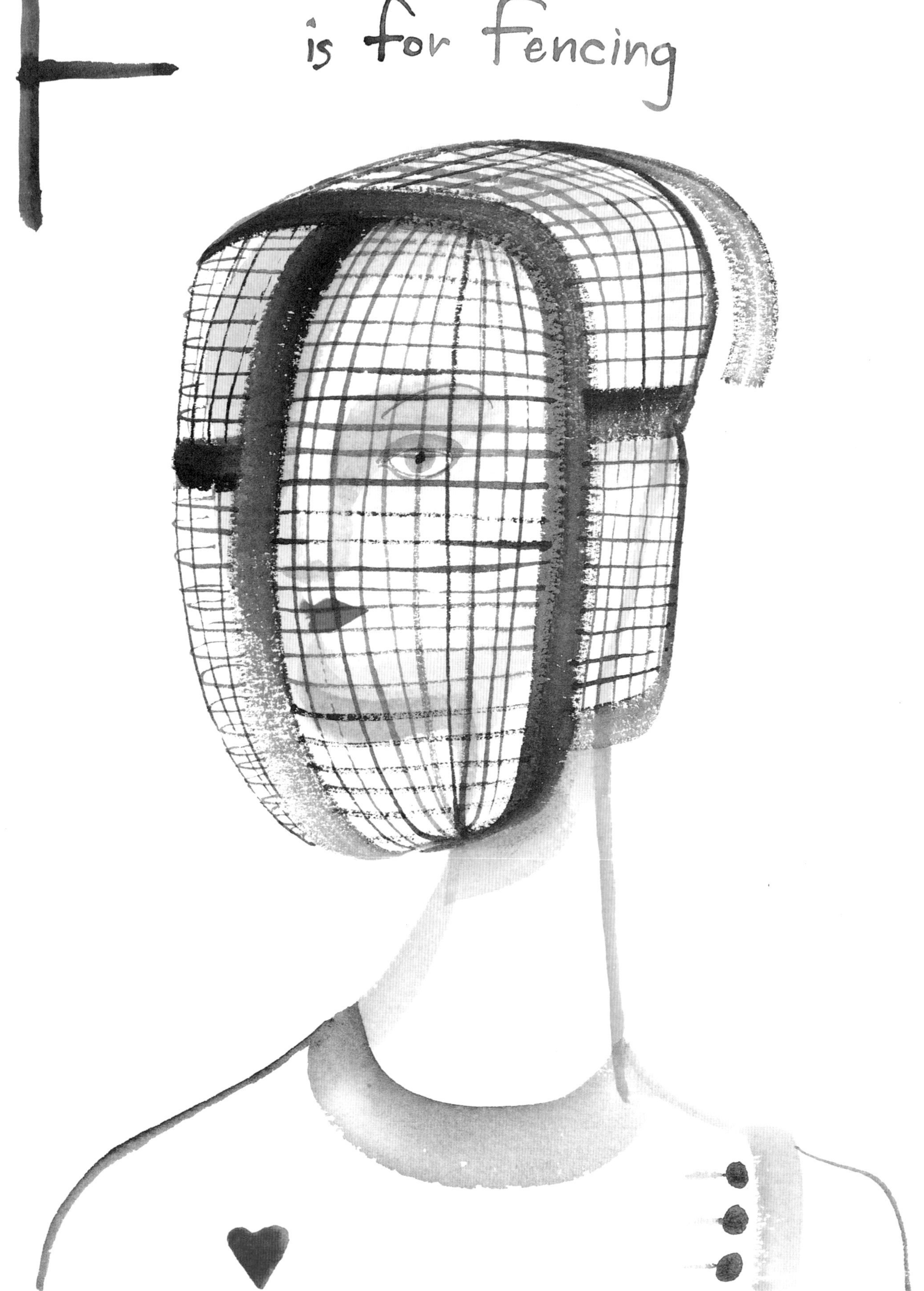
F
is for fencing

F is for farthingale
Fan Feathers
FeZ
Faces
optimistic
pessimistic
Agonistic
ALtruistic

G is for Gypsy

H is
for hair

H is for High Heel

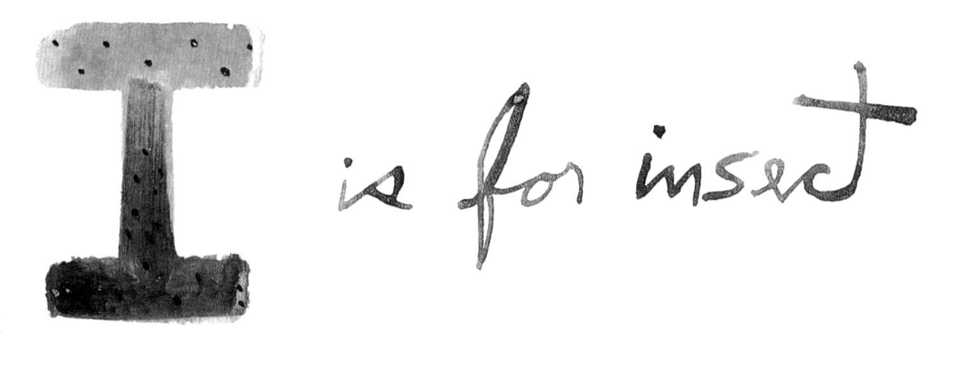
I is for insect

........and also InFANTA

j is for jacket (a unisex garment)

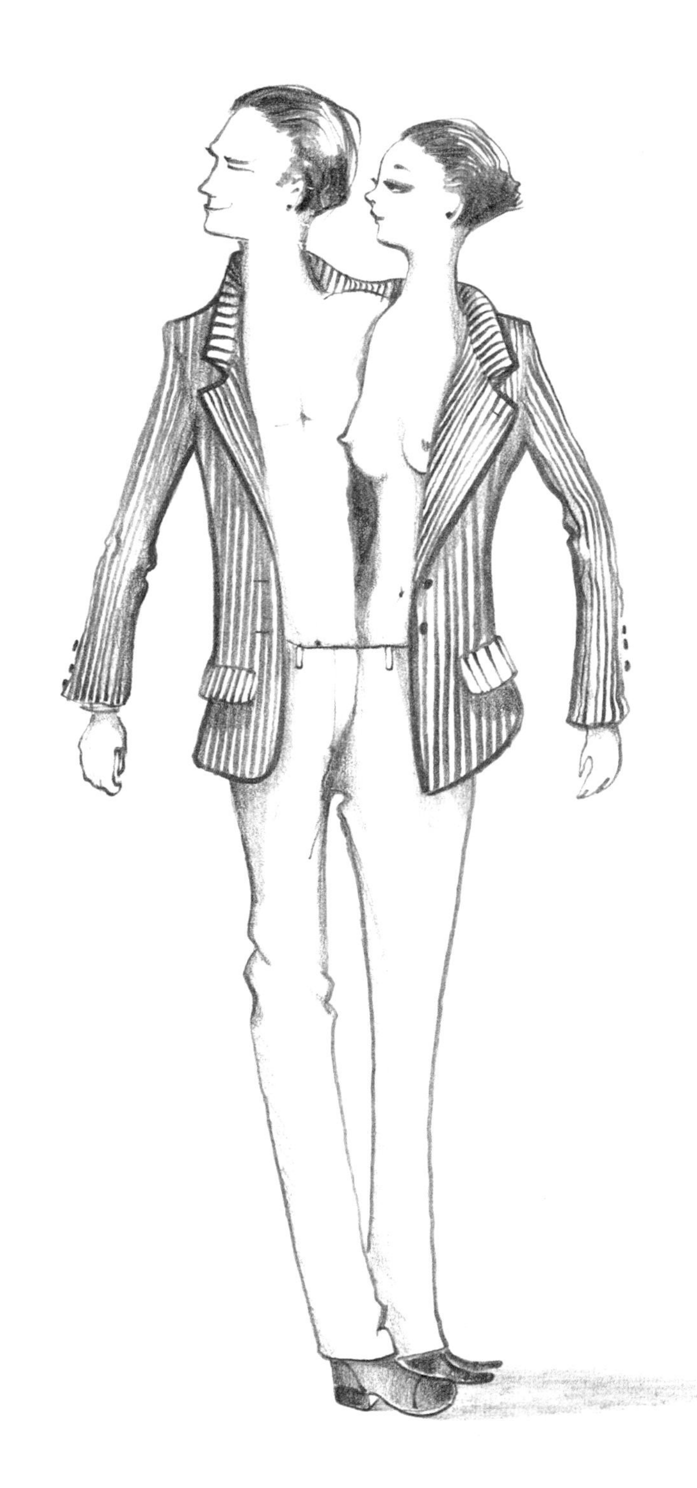

K
is for
KIMONO

L IS FOR Lapel

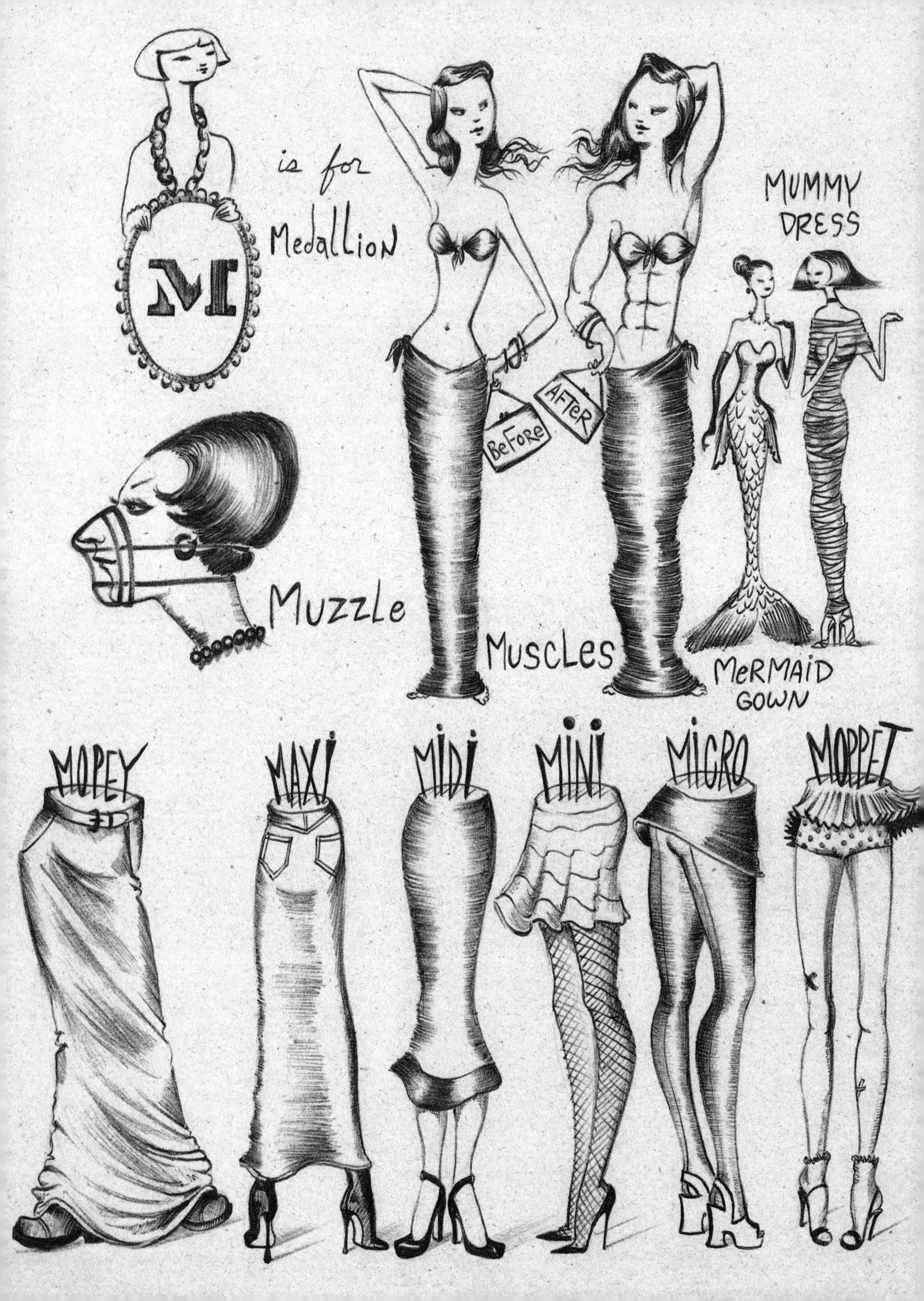
M
is for
Medallion
Muzzle
BeFore
AFTeR
Muscles
MUMMY DRESS
MeRMAID GOWN
MOPEY
MAXI
MIDI
MINI
MICRO
MOPPET

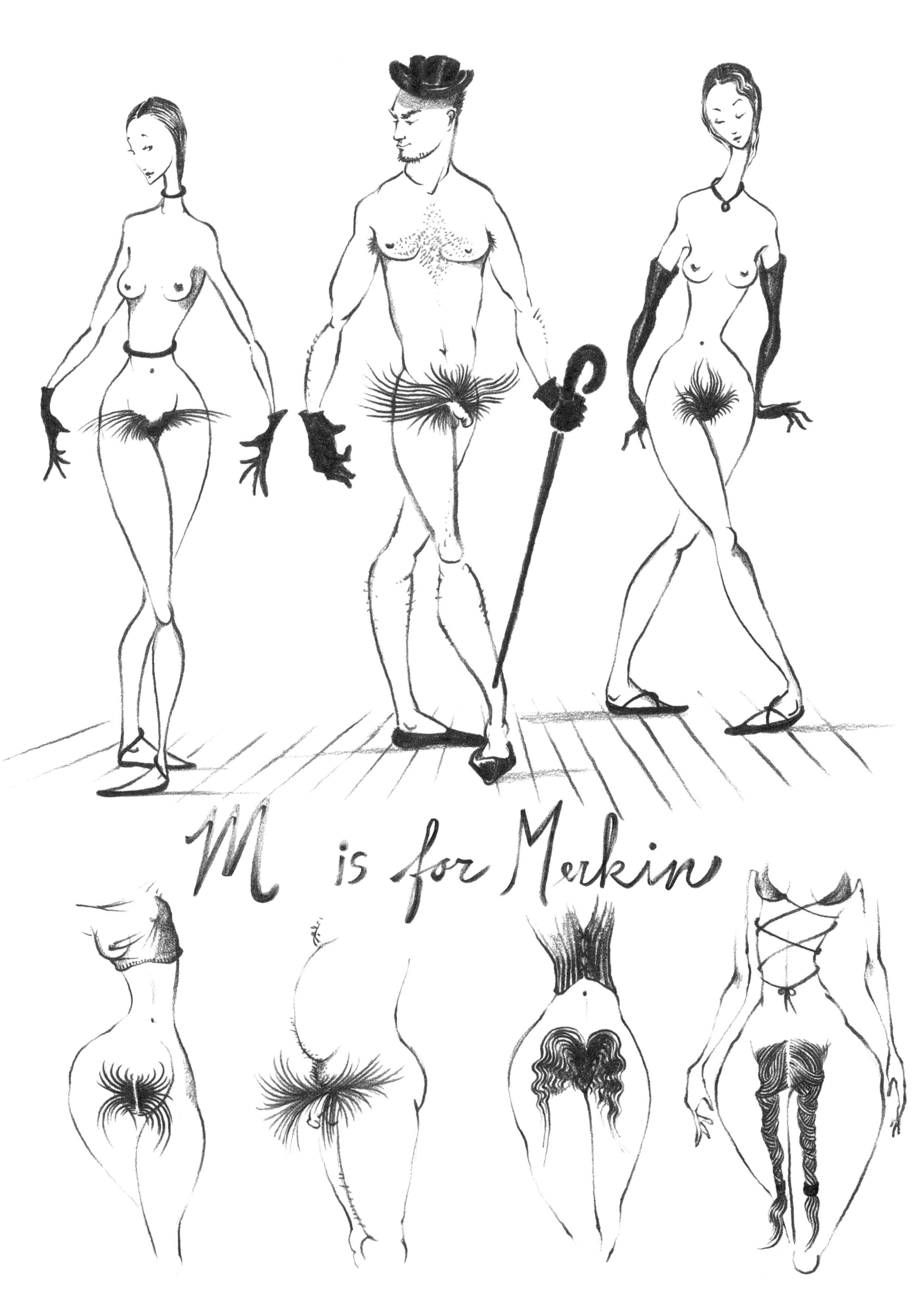
M is for Merkin

N
Nun
Nymph

Nurse
Nightgown

O is for ostrich

P is for PANTS

Q IS FOR DRAGQUEEN,

TRADITIONALIST *Contemporary* COUNTER-CULTURE

Raver
Racoon makeup
Raw Hide
rasta
ROYAList
ruffLe
Ring
Master

S is for

1885 1958 1818 1902

SILHOUETTe
1922
1872

1840

is for S-curve
SHoulders
SHoulder-pad
SHoulderette
SHOULDER BLADES
QUARTer-Back
Leg-of-Mutton
10
Running back
Weeping-Willow
SHawls

Toreador
Toga
Tattoo
talisman
Turtle - Neck

T is FOR TeXTURE

U
is
for
U
Ni
fo
RM

U is for umbrella

V is for victory

W is for Wigs
The unfaithful
the indiscrete
the 400 BLOWS
the great shock
the perfect CanDour
the MATRON within
the oh-so-SATisfied
the come and see
the early American
the No Regrets
the Neo-pagan
the Brutus
the UN-ANNOUNCED
the bridge and tunnel
the devil may care
the who-me?

X
is for extra Large

PINK DRED-LOCKS

BOWS IN HAIR

Y

cut offs

is for **youth**

ARMY PANTS

MUDD

CK
ME

EAT
YOUR
PARENTS
OPEN
YOUR
MIND

PORNO
BOY
PULL
MY
DAISY

U.S.A.
U.O.K.
U.F.O
Les
Be
FrieNDs

DAME

FUN
GUS
HOUSE-FRAU
OF
THIS
WORLD
NOT

DROP-WAIST

Little girl dresses ←

SLIPS SHOWING ←

POWER
U.S.!
ACT UP
MY BOD

FETUS

GREEN TIPS ON BLOND

FLASHER RAINCOATS

EAR PLUGS
MOM

SPA
NOT
POP

?
in-voice

ICE

BLUE BANGS
BLACK-BOB
GRANDMA'S
HOUSE DRESS
MESH STOCKINGS
70'S
PLASTIC SHOE
Boy
HAIR CUT
with
BLACK
ENDS
PENCIL
MOUSTACHE
ON GIRL
DAISY
DECAL
T-
SHIRT
TUCKED
INTO
BRA
ROLLED
STRAPS
Belt on
Waist
CUT
OFF
JEANS
MESH
Knee-Highs

Z is for zipper . . . !

SCENES—SEVENTH AVENUE AND BEYOND

Design for shopping bag. 1988

Summer fashion. 1988

Farmers almanac predicts a good straw harvest and a bad fabric shortage! *Details*, June 1988

City pavement will be tickled this season. *Details*, 1988

Fashion freedom fighters take manufacturer hostage! *Details*, June/July 1988

Portrait of Frank DeCaro, fashion journalist *N.Y. Post. Visionaire,* 1989

Confused customers give up clothes and start wearing fashion magazines! *Details*, July 1988

Seventh Ave. says women will wear nothing but pants this fall season. *Details*, August 1988

Fashion archaeology: Stepping back into the future. *Taxi Magazine,* May 1983

Fashion history goes on strike! *Details*, September 1988

Animation project for "Seventh Ave. Opera." Animated film, 1991

Proposal for reconstruction of New York City's Seventh Ave., "Fashion Ave." 1988

Proposal for renovation of 42 St.–"Times Square renovation project"
Buildings will serve their purpose in the future. 1989

Fear of shopping on Madison Ave., attitude shopping. *Vogue,* March 1989

Seventh Ave. welcomes back fashion buyers. *Details*, November 1988

On sale now—designer Christmas trees. *Details*, December 1988

Wall Street fashion forecast for fiscal year 1988. *Wall Street Journal,* 1988

The Kiss. Cover for Bal De L'Amour catalog. Paris, 1992

Surgeon General's warning: Prolonged use of stretch fabric may be dangerous to your hips, thighs, breasts and buttocks. *Details*, October 1988

High fashion merchandise attacks potential customers! *Details*, April 1989

Seventh Ave. hopes to harvest a new crop of designs this spring. *Details*, March 1989

You are what you eat. *Details,* 1989

You are what you eat [2]. *Details,* 1989

Women may choose to wear their fashion statements this season. *Details*, May 1989

Seventh Ave. introduces new swimwear for today's beaches. *Details*, June/July 1989

Untitled
Esquire, 1988

Men's fashion helps tame the beast. *Details*, September 1989

Seventh Ave. now faces the challenge of designing for the modern woman. *Details*, September 1989

Portrait of Isabel. March 1982

High fashion under high security at a retail shop near you! *Details*, October 1989

Geoffrey Beene dress. *Taxi Magazine,* 1989

Endangered animals turn the tables on Seventh Ave. *Details*, November 1989

Mickey Mouse meets high fashion. 1991

Seventh Ave. wraps up the decade with the spirit of giving. *Details*, December 1989

The shape of things to come on Seventh Ave. *Details*, February 1990

Women I have known (a fashion story; Sawdust Twins) *Details*, 1988

Women I have known (a fashion story; Marina) *Details*, 1988

Women I have known (a fashion story; Angelina) *Details*, 1988

Women I have known (a fashion story; Rose) *Details*, 1988

Untitled
Visionaire, 1991

Some women will choose to shed their shells this spring. *Details*, March 1990

"High fashion" California style. *Details*, March 1990

Catalog for exhibition, "Modes et Libertés," Musée des Arts de La Mode et du Textile, Paris. July 1992

AIDS changes the face of Seventh Ave. *Details*, May 1990

Creativity walks the plank on Seventh Ave. *Details*, February 1989

A first in publishing history—Fashion magazine gets a sex-change! *Details*, June 1990

DETAILS
DETAILS
DETAIL
Details

DESIGN FOR SHOPPING BAG. *1988*

SUMMER FASHION. *1988*

FARMERS ALMANAC PREDICTS A GOOD STRAW HARVEST AND A BAD FABRIC SHORTAGE

Details, June 1988

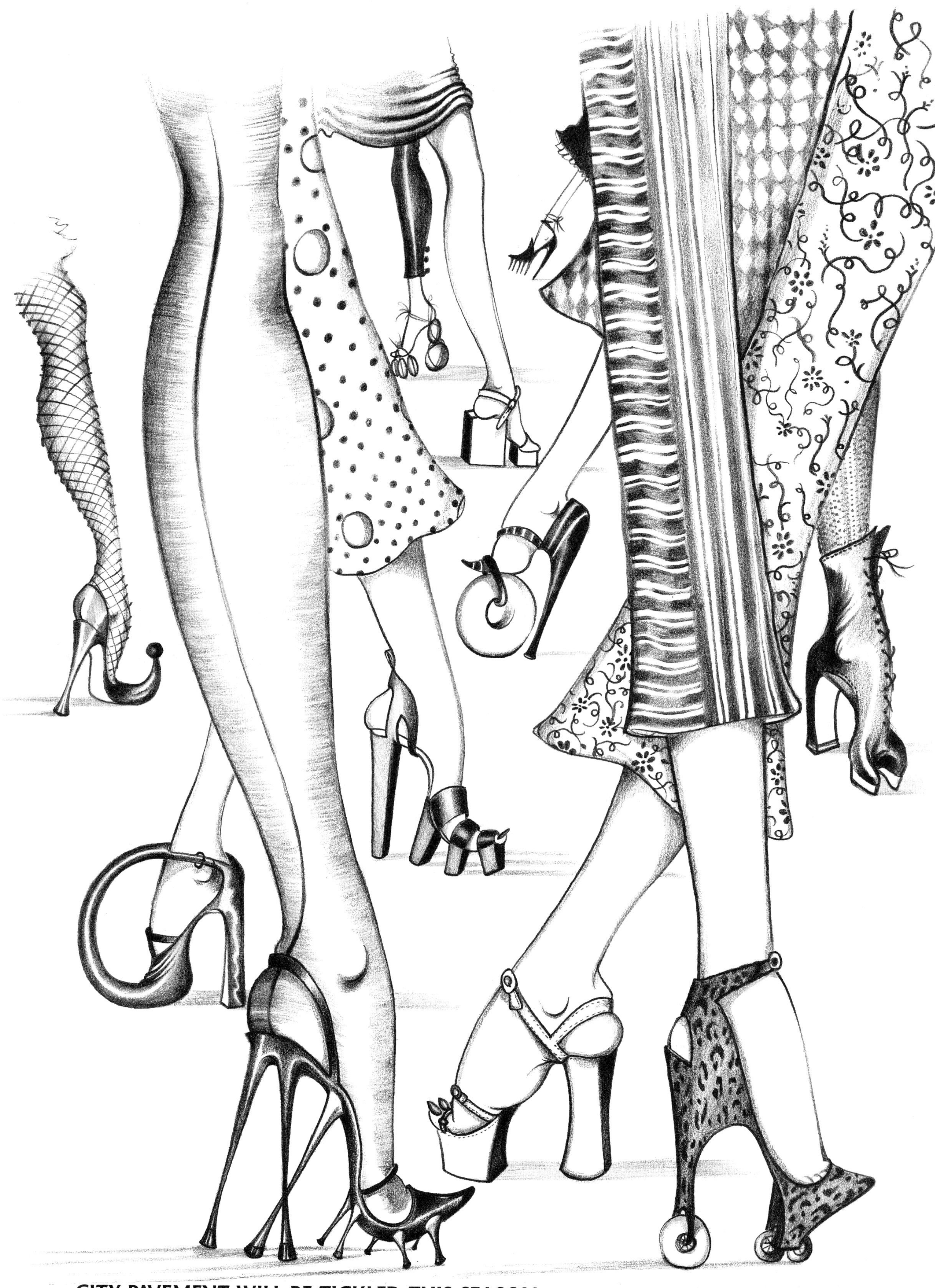

CITY PAVEMENT WILL BE TICKLED THIS SEASON. *Details, 1988*

FASHION FREEDOM FIGHTERS TAKE MANUFACTURER HOSTAGE! *Details, June & July 1988*

PORTRAIT OF FRANK DeCARO, FASHION JOURNALIST N.Y. POST. *Visionaire 1989*

CONFUSED CUSTOMERS GIVE UP CLOTHES AND START WEARING FASHION MAGAZINES! *Details, July 1988*

7TH AVE. SAYS WOMEN WILL WEAR NOTHING BUT PANTS THIS FALL SEASON. *Details, August 1988*

FASHION ARCHAEOLOGY: STEPPING BACK INTO THE FUTURE. *Taxi Magazine, May 1983*

FASHION HISTORY GOES ON STRIKE! *Details, September 1988*

ANIMATION PROJECT FOR "7TH AVE. OPERA". *Animation film, 1991*

PROPOSAL FOR RECONSTRUCTION OF NEW YORK CITY'S SEVENTH AVE., "FASHION AVE." *1988*

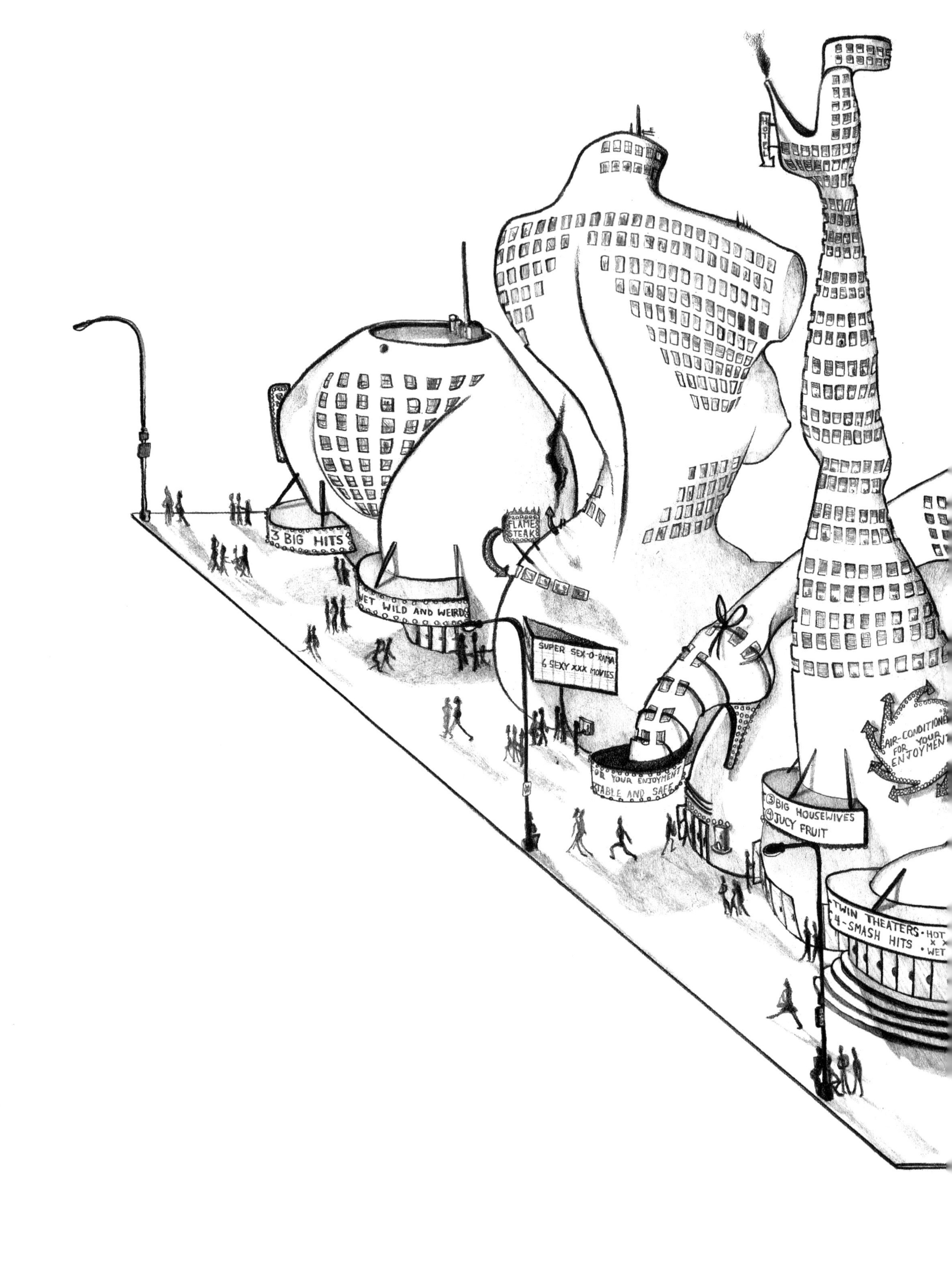

PROPOSAL FOR RENOVATION OF 42ST. - "TIMES SQUARE RENOVATION PROJECT" BUILDINGS

WILL SERVE THEIR PURPOSE IN THE FUTURE. *1989*

FEAR OF SHOPPING ON MADISON AVE., ATTITUDE SHOPPING.

Vogue, March 1989

7TH AVE. WELCOMES BACK FASHION BUYERS. *Details, November 1988*

ON SALE NOW -
DESIGNER CHRISTMAS TREES.
Details, December 1988

WALL STREET FASHION FORECAST FOR FISCAL YEAR 1988.

Wall Street Journal, 1988

THE KISS.
Cover for Bal De L'Amour Catalog, Paris, 1992

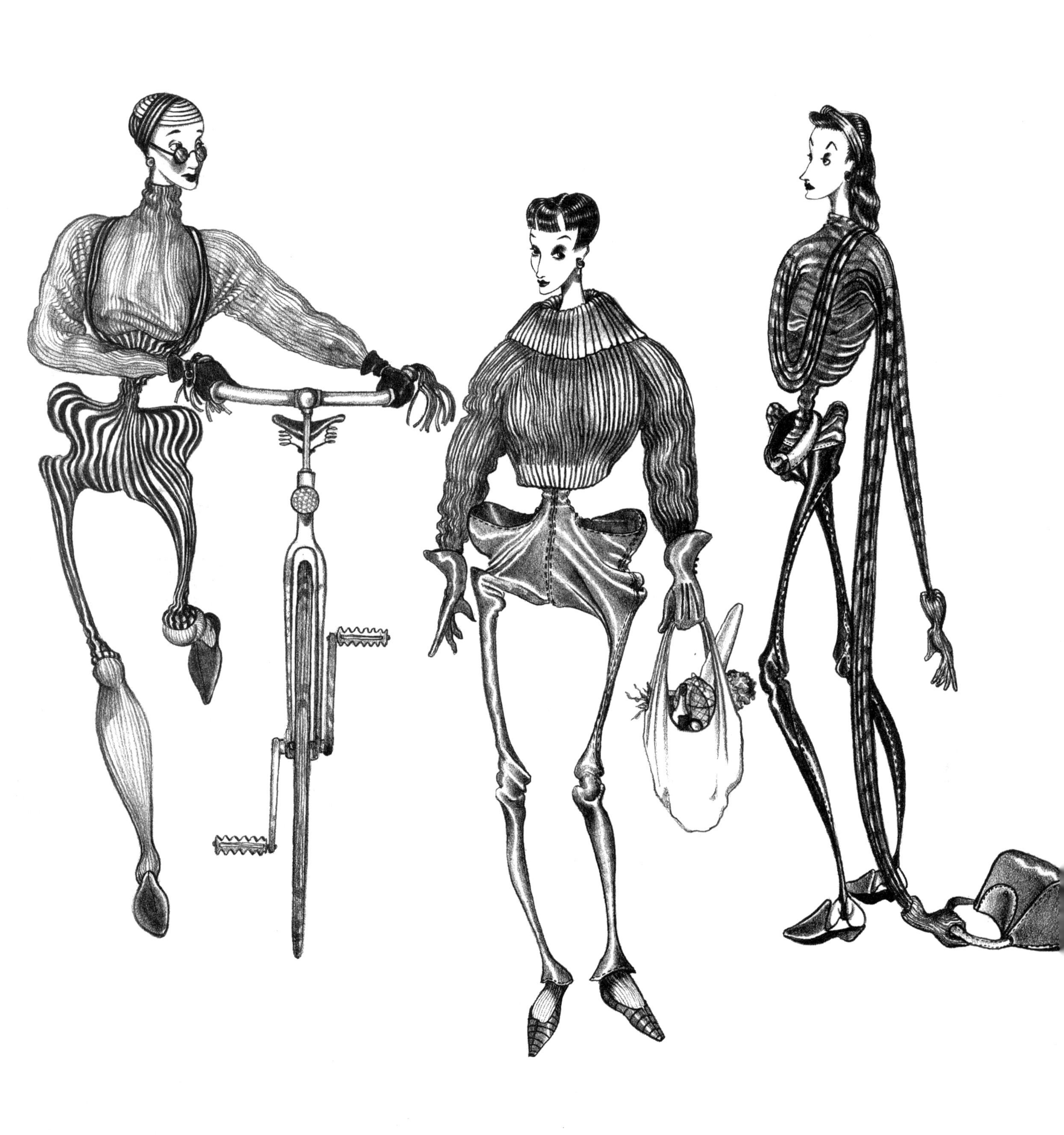

SURGEON GENERAL'S WARNING: PROLONGED USE OF STRETCH FABRIC MAY BE DANGEROUS TO YOUR HIPS, THIGHS, BREASTS & BUTTOCKS.

Details, October 1988

HIGH FASHION MERCHANDISE ATTACKS POTENTIAL CUSTOMERS!

Details, April 1989

FASHION AV
7 AV
HOME-GROWN
AMERICAN
FASHIONS
BUYERS
WELCOME

7TH AVE. HOPES TO HARVEST A NEW CROP OF DESIGNS THIS SPRING. *Details, March 1989*

YOU ARE WHAT YOU EAT.
Details 1989

YOU ARE WHAT YOU EAT.
Details 1989

WOMEN MAY CHOOSE TO WEAR THEIR FASHION STATEMENTS THIS SEASON. *Details, May 1989*

7TH AVE. INTRODUCES NEW SWIMWEAR FOR TODAY'S BEACHES. *Details, June/July 1989*

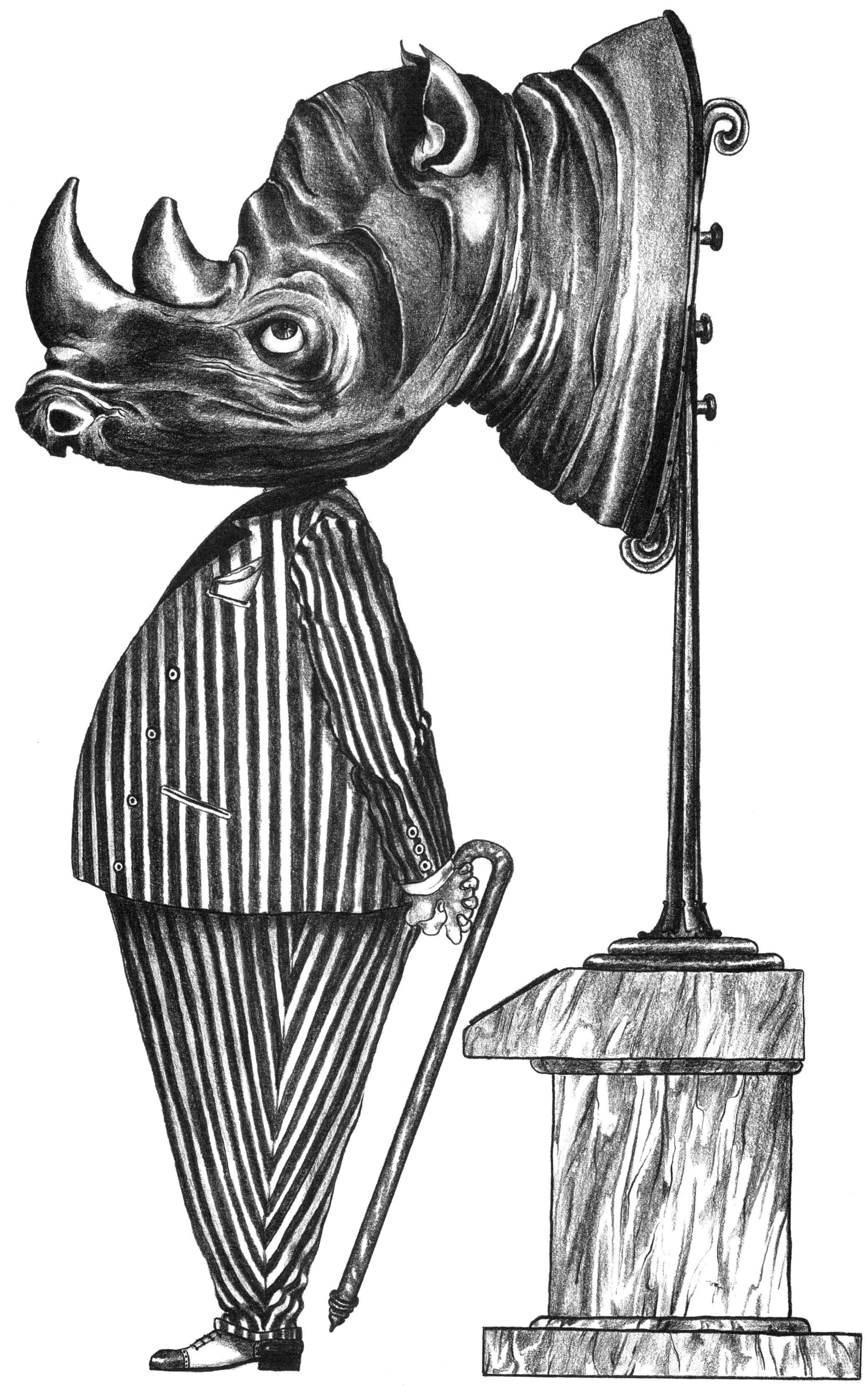

Esquire, 1988

MEN'S FASHION HELPS TAME THE BEAST. *Details, September 1989*

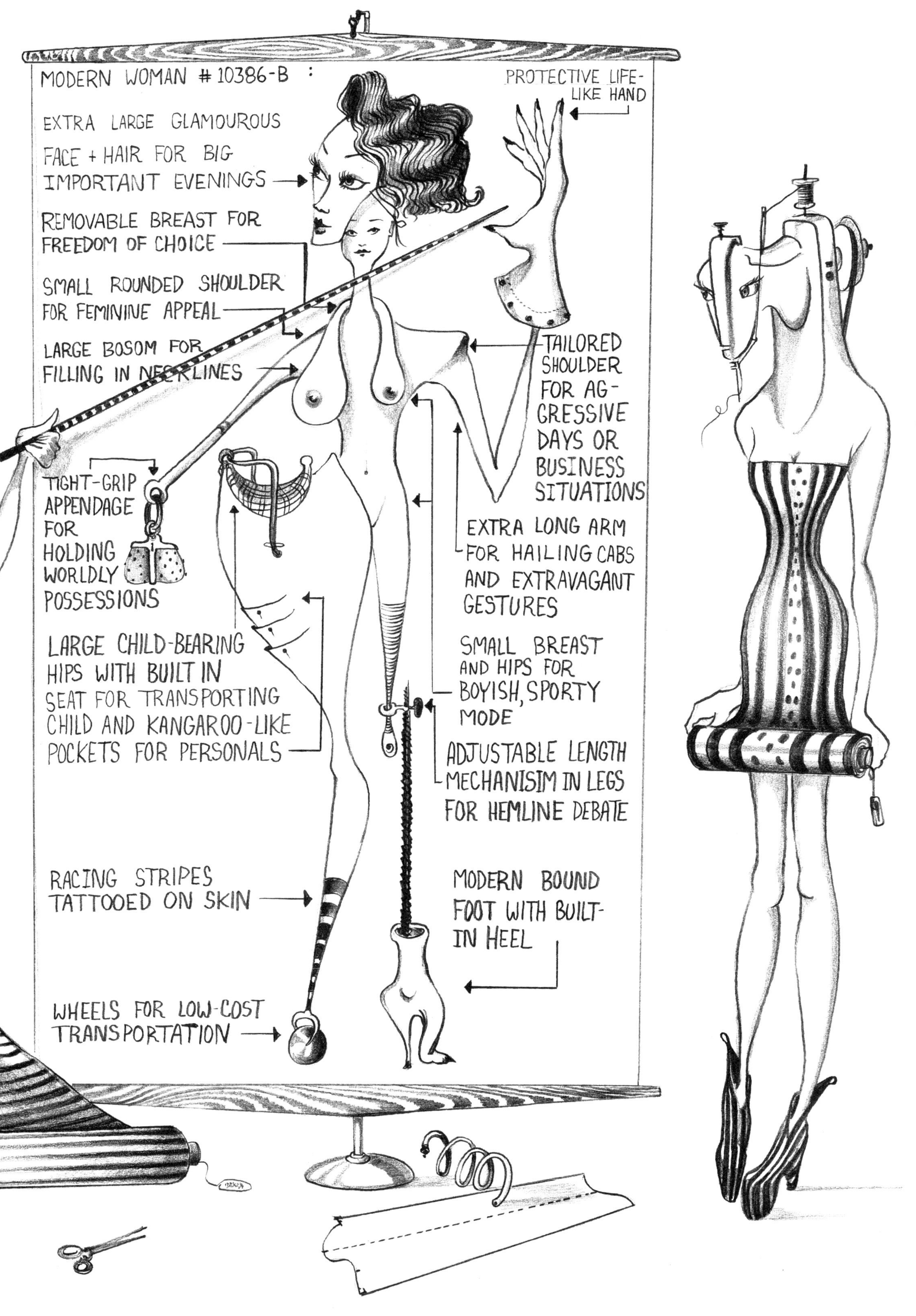

7TH AVE. NOW FACES THE CHALLENGE OF DESIGNING FOR THE MODERN WOMAN.

Details, September 1989

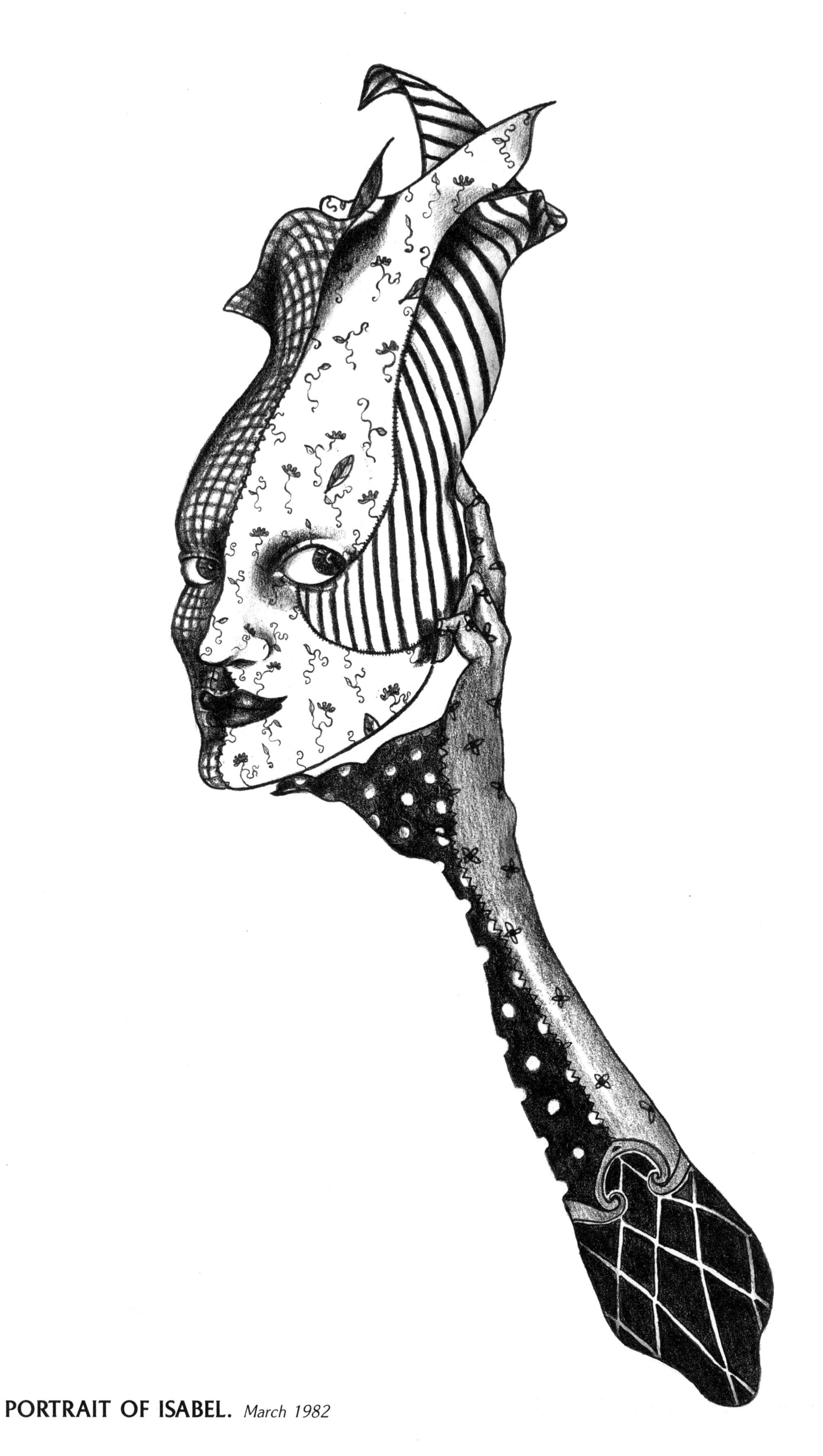

PORTRAIT OF ISABEL. *March 1982*

HIGH FASHION UNDER HIGH SECURITY AT A RETAIL SHOP NEAR YOU! *Details, October 1989*

GEOFFREY BEENE DRESS. *Taxi Magazine, 1989*

ENDANGERED ANIMALS TURN THE TABLES ON SEVENTH AVE. *Details, November 1989*

MICKEY MOUSE MEETS HIGH FASHION. *1991*

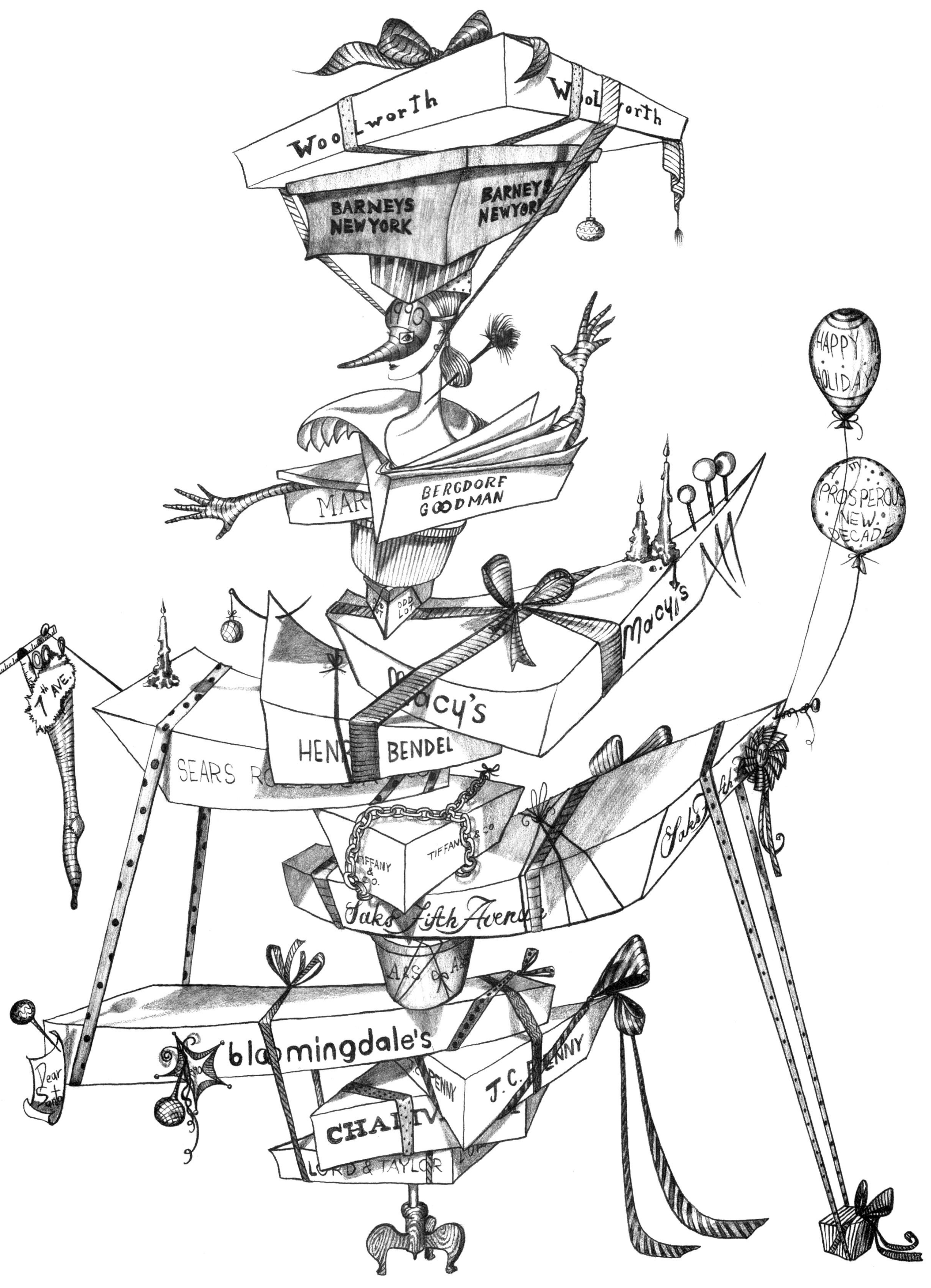

7TH AVE. WRAPS UP THE DECADE WITH THE SPIRIT OF GIVING. *Details, December 1989*

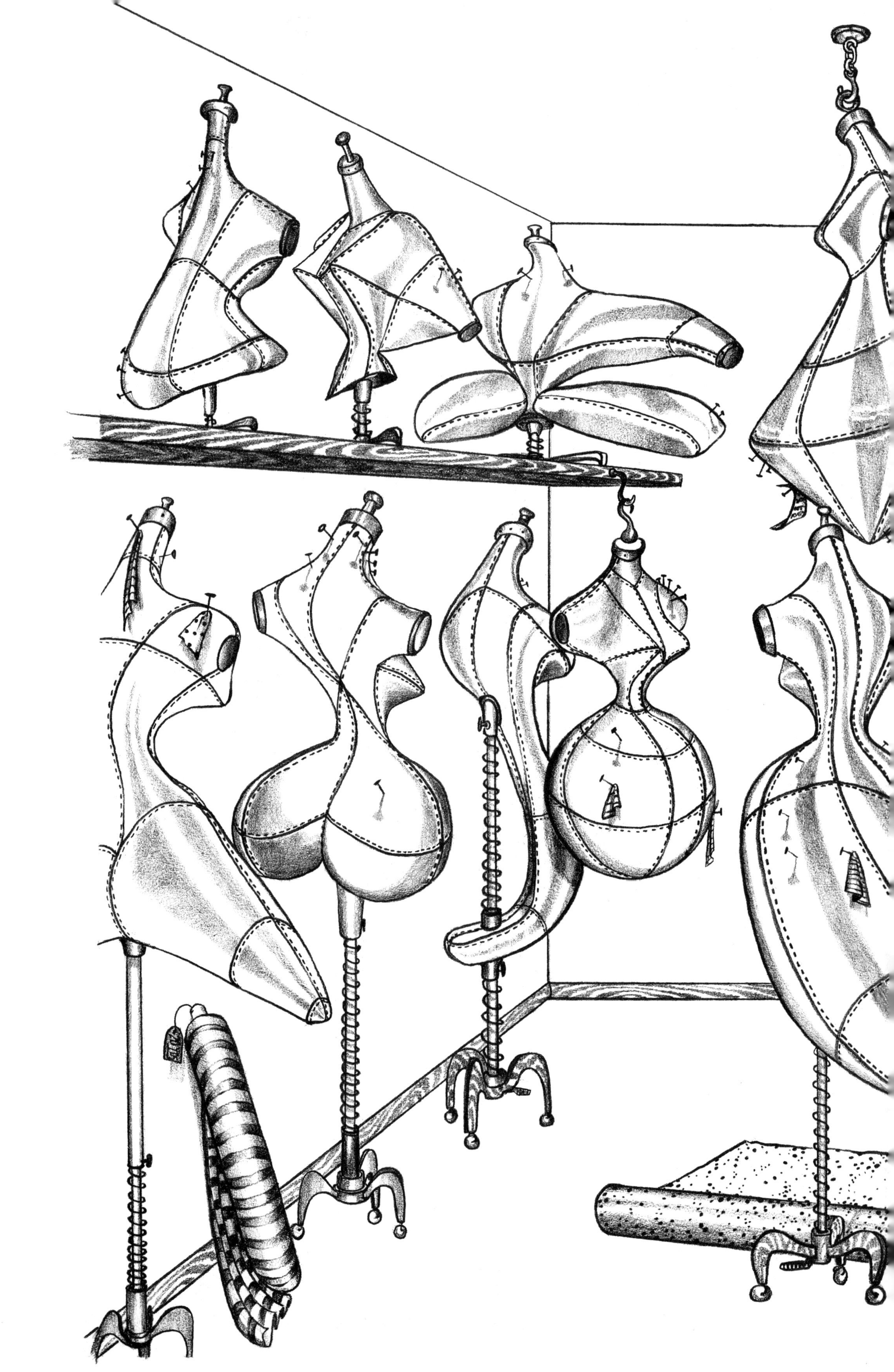

THE SHAPE OF THINGS TO COME ON 7TH AVE. *Details, February 1990*

THE SAWDUST TWINS WERE MY FIRST LOVE - I NEVER COULD CHOOSE BETWEEN THEM AND THAT SORT OF RUBBED AGAINST THEIR GRAIN ...

Details, 1988

I THOUGHT MARINA WAS QUITE A CATCH - BUT MY FRIENDS ALWAYS KNEW THERE WAS SOMETHING FISHY ABOUT HER ...

Details, 1988

ANGELINA WAS A HEAVENLY BODY! BUT I WAS NOT DOWN TO EARTH ENOUGH FOR HER ...

Details, 1988

THE MOST FERTILE WOMAN I EVER MET WAS ROSE - A PURE LONG STEM AMERICAN BEAUTY! OUR SEASON TOGETHER WAS BRIEF - OUR ROMANCE SOON WILTED ...

Details, 1988

Visionaire, 1991

SOME WOMEN WILL CHOOSE TO SHED THEIR SHELLS THIS SPRING. *Details, March 1990*

"HIGH FASHION" CALIFORNIA STYLE. *Details, March 1990*

Catalog for exhibition; "Mode et Libertés", Musée des Arts de La Mode et du Textile, Paris. Costume by Martin Margiela, July 1992

AIDS CHANGES THE FACE OF 7TH AVE. *Details, May 1990*

CREATIVITY WALKS THE PLANK ON 7TH AVE. *Details, February 1989*

A FIRST IN PUBLISHING HISTORY - FASHION MAGAZINE GETS A SEX-CHANGE! *Details, June 1990*

Concept design: Juan E. Ramos.
Book design, original Japanese edition: Koichi Yoshida, and Shelter & Graphic Associates.

Inquiries should be addressed to Abbeville Publishing Group, 488 Madison Avenue, New York, N.Y. 10022. Printed and bound in Japan. ISBN 0-7892-0348-0
First edition

10 9 8 7 6 5 4 3 2 1

SPECIAL THANKS TO: PAUL CARANICAS, JOEY ARIAS, BETTINA, SIMON DOONAN, WENDY GOODMAN, ADELINE ANDRE, STEVAN DOHAR, KACHIN, RUVEN AFANADOR, HAROLD KODA, KIM HASTREITER AND GLORIA, CHRISTIAN LÉVÊQUE, MARTIN MARGIELA, ANNELIESE ESTRADA, OLGA VEJVODA, MAUD MOLYNEUX, JUNKO OUCHI, SUZANNE BARTSCH, FLORENCE MÜLLER, ORLANDO PITA, AYA MIYAUCHI, BENJAMIN LIU, STEPHEN GAN, GEANE BRITO, OLIVIER GUILLEMIN, BILL CUNNINGHAM, LADY BUNNY, CHRISTIAN LACROIX,

CAROL RAMER, TERRY & LOUISE DOKTOR, ANNIE FLANDERS, WOODY HOCHSWENDER, SYLVIE GRUMBACH, NANCY GALLAGHER, FRANCK JOSEPH BASTILLE, HOLLY BRUBACH, ALEX GONZALES, TODD OLDHAM, KATSUKO YAMADA, CECILIA DEAN, ANGELICA STEUDEL, BOO, SUZIE ZABROWSKA, GENE PRESSMAN, JAMES KALIARDOS, MANOLO BLAHNIK, GEORGE MALKEMUS III, FRANS ANKONE, MIKE SILVERSTEIN, KENNY SCHARF, MIN + OLI SANCHEZ, ANGEL DORMER, CHINO + WOODY, VICTORIA BARTLET, BETHANN, TED MUEHLING, GORAN VEJVODA, MATS GUSTAFSON, GREG MILLS, RALPH PUCCI, YUKO ARAKAWA, SUZETTE, MRS. PATER SATO, VALERIE STEELE, THE BARONESS, LITA, TERESA STEWART, NAO OISHI + CHARLES MANZO, TAIKO & ASSOCIATES, MUSÉE DES ARTS DE LA MODE ET DU TEXTILE